First edition published May, 2012

ISBN # 978-1-105-78910-6

Preface

This book acts as a reminder based on practical experiences and understanding of something that we move continuously in our lives with, called change and something that we fear to take, that is, the first step. It is about understanding ourselves clearly & others in the process of making a way from where we are, & where we want to be.

You get to know about breaking open the barriers that hold us back from making progress in life & how to conquer them. You get quick insights on how you can lead in life and climb the ladder of success. Written with absolute simplicity, this book will act as a tool of understanding & finding solutions pointing towards the better side of your existence.

This book is dedicated to some of my closest friends & family, who have been the inspiration behind writing this book.

Without them, this book could not have been a reality.

Table of Contents

The Journey Starts With a Step

"Every step taken is the result of the change we want to make in our lives and every step taken also results in the change that we want to see in our lives."

~Sahil Sharma

Full of billions of people, this world carries a number of personalities, behaviors, attitudes and perspectives. But not everyone seeks change. Ask yourself for your own reaction, if you would be transferred to a village-like smaller place from cities like Vancouver or New York. Would you accept it easily? The human nature is such that it does not accept change that easily. It gets agitated and shows resistance to break the comfortable silk cocoon it has been hiding in. Although, it wants to become a butterfly but being a caterpillar sounds like a safe idea to it.

"Change is the safest place to be in."

~Sahil Sharma

We have to remember that taking the first step towards doing anything that is desired stems from a process called "change". A person who wants to take the first step in achieving his desires is basically looking for a change in his present existence of life. A stagnant life will leave you behind and move on. When you decide to change with time, you'll always feel more comfortable in life. Everything seems to walk with you because you decide to walk with them. It's a mutual understanding with time.

"I "Want a Change

"I the change to see We the change."

~Sahil Sharma

Remember in life that it is not others who need to change for you but it is mostly you who has to change to experience the change. It clearly means that we need to work on ourselves to have a better life that we have imagined for ourselves. The moment you are able to say with a self reflective affirmation, “I want a change”, the “I” transforms into and stands for “individuality”. This individuality comes with some aspects:

- Acceptance of who you are and the uniqueness that comes with it;
- Responsibility of making the change that is desired;
- Honesty towards your own self and breaking the false images that might be reflecting ego;
- Believing in yourself;
- Willingness to create change;
- Commitment to stick on to the path not just physically but emotionally as well;
- Focusing on the bigger picture or the purpose.

A person who finds his individuality will be known as an individual.

More to Walk Before You Run

I see the light within me as bright as the sun that can shine the entire world in its existence."

~Sahil Sharma

It is very important for every person to know about himself. Introspection comes handy when you are thinking of a change. Before we move ahead, let me give you an example. Have you ever stopped and noticed the old picture that has been hanging on your house wall for the last 10 years? Have you tried stopping and noticed, how many steps do you take every day to get down from the house to the road? I bet, never.

We are so much involved in thoughts that distract us every second of our lives about things that we don't have or the things that we desire that we forget what we actually have. I have a little story to share here.

I was spending a day with an old friend of mine. We sat on the computer and we were going through some things randomly within the computer. There was a folder named, "videos". My friend was curious enough to see what was inside. I told him with less interest that it had some old videos that I had shot earlier. He insisted on watching some of them. I played them for him and went to the kitchen, thinking that I should utilize this time in getting something to eat than watching the same thing over and over again.

When I came back, he asked, “Who made these videos?”

“I did”, I said.

“Where did you learn to do all this video editing and taking all these angles and shots?” Digging in to the conversation, he asked.

“Let’s have this yummy chicken and kebab rolls that I have for you, my friend. Come let’s eat.” I said.

His inquisitive mind was still into the videos, he went on. “Umm…you have some great skills and I would be glad to have you as a part of my organization. Why don’t you think about it?”

“Skills? Are you kidding me? It’s just my passion. I just do it for fun. I thought every organization wants people with certificates and big names attached to them. It sounds weird coming from you that I could contribute with all this”, I said.

Later that day when he left, I kept thinking about everything that happened and at 2 AM went out of my bed and landed in front of the computer to watch my videos again. However, this time my eyes were looking at something different. I wasn't watching the same old videos, but the work that I had done with passion. As if, I just saw them for the very first time. I even started noticing things that I could change to make them better. I felt like Steven Spielberg with all the enormous shots that he takes and the sounds were fluttering into my ears; Cut! Perfect! Let's do this again! Let's take the other angle!

The whole episode with my friend changed my self-perception. I started remembering making little videos out of mobile phones and then using the free or trial versions of various software to make little clips that I called my little movies. I wasn't bad at all and way better than the utter crap that I saw on the local stations many a times.

The example above clearly shows that a lot of times we do not notice what's inside us because we take our talents and skills for granted. We need a fresh pair of eyes, or a refreshed vision to look into all of that and then see what is actually present.

Putting Yourself on a Piece of Paper Can Make You a Picasso

Human beings are visual beings; at least that's what I notice in my experience of life. Then why not write some things down on a piece of paper about yourself and see how you are doing for a change?

A technique that never goes unnoticed and used at every level to self reflect is called "SWOT". I had learnt this in high school, then in my university and finally, have been using this technique during my training sessions. It has always helped open newer perspectives in myself and also, in others. I am sure that many of you know about it and use it in your offices and projects. Now, how about using it personally? All you need to do is SWOT yourself down. It is not a shame or something to ignore. Most of us would hesitate doing it for ourselves thinking that we know ourselves well. The question is- Really?

S: Strengths – Your virtues
W: Weaknesses – The gaps
O: Opportunities- Your possibilities
T: Threats- The known unknown

The moment you figure these out, you will have a much clearer picture of yourself.

Strengths are like your virtues. Looking and utilizing what you have is what you have to focus on. For example, knowing an extra language, being organized, being a problem solver, knowing computers very well, being creative, being academically excellent, being a singer, dancer, musician, being an excellent salesman, and so much more.

Weaknesses are like gaps; things that may not work out to be strong enough. These aren't your fault that you have to be guilty about. These are the things that were left behind a bit and have the absolute potential of overcoming. For example, being short tempered, not having a certain skill that acts as a hindrance in moving forward, being unorganized, etc.

Opportunities are gifts to be availed from life that have not yet been redeemed. Look at your weaknesses and change them into opportunities to cover those gaps and work on yourself. For example, you could work on managing your anger through anger management activities, or go to school to learn a skill that can help you move forward in life.

Threats are the earthquakes. They are the external factors that may or may not affect you at some point. But you have to be ready for them. For example, you have to move from your country or a place due to some special unforeseen circumstances, or being in an accident suddenly that leaves you disabled to go back to work or business.

This is how you paint your own picture correctly and also, make an honest confession to yourself. SWOT it!

You See It, Now That You Know It!

After confessing to yourself about your being, you must either be very excited or very disappointed. Most likely, your weaknesses must have disappointed you. However, the right approach should be towards the happiness of finding weaknesses that can be worked upon and shifted in the section of your virtues.

Starting out with a positive outlook is very important. Since you are seeking a change or want to take the first step towards what you desire, you are able to see better, how much of what you can do for yourself in order to achieve that change.

Still, there is a little more investigation left for you to do. Remember, everyone in this life wants change for their betterment but the whole idea of change needs a direction backed up by your motives and results desired.

That means we all need a direction to convert our intentions or motives into our desired results.

Now, we have some very important questions to be answered.

You Ask Questions & You Know the Answer

"Before you start some work, always ask yourself three questions - Why am I doing it, what the results might be and will I be successful. Only when you think deeply and find satisfactory answers to these questions, go ahead."

~Chanakya

Every person who is seeking change has different motives and desired results in mind to achieve. For example, an ex CEO of a well reputed corporation, who has earned billions of dollars throughout his career might want to take early retirement and start his own social enterprise to help out the needy because he feels now that he needs ___________.

Another example could be about a young man who has been doing 9 to 5 jobs for several years and probably is bored and wants to do something different in life that can give him ____________.
I have left those blanks above for you to think at first, what these two personalities must be trying to seek.

The common answers would include desiring anything out of things like money, a better house, bigger status, easy life, being their own boss, excitement in life and more.

However, every one of us ultimately is seeking change to achieve only and only one thing. It is called "happiness". You could very well fill the blanks up there with this word.

I asked this gentleman who is an ex CEO of a huge corporation the reason why he took early retirement and started his own social enterprise to help youth and make them employable through training. He answered, "I had seen it all. Initially I thought, having bigger cars, house, and handsome salary can keep me happy. Then people thought the same about me. After that I realized that I was missing out on something. There was something that I wanted to do but could never do. I wanted to help. I realized years after that I worked like a robot to make myself and my family happy through money. We all know but never understand the point here. This social enterprise gives me much more satisfaction and happiness when I go back home at the end of every day empowering the needy. My pockets are not so full any more but it enlightens me."

Therefore, the example tells us that anyone who seeks a change in life has a desire for happiness in its respective forms. Therefore, the question of "why" has been answered.

The question about what the results might be and achieving success as a result of your change is critical. A thousand questions may arise at this moment starting from "what if".

Moving Ahead With Heart, Mind & the Rest

"Imagination sounds great but practicality matters. Always work for a way, where they meet.
~Sahil Sharma

Anyone who has even self reflected and has a dream to achieve his desires comes to a standstill at this very point. But the best thing is that there is clarity about your own self. Confession has been made.

A very good friend of mine, who has been a radio broadcaster and a social worker for more than a decade, is a great example to share.

She had an imagination to help out people, while working for her own self. A ton of ideas rolled down her mind every day. But it was critical to do something that was practically possible and effective.

She had already looked inside her. The gold was separated from silver and bronze. She shared her dream with the people she could trust and the ones that could contribute. With all the resources in place; human and material, she successfully started her own media based social enterprise. Its weekly television project won its first community award in only 4 months of its existence and has been nominated in several others. This social enterprise has helped a lot of talented youth in getting recognition in what they are good at. It has helped fill the gap between generations. It also helped youth focus on their abilities, rather than getting attracted towards violence, crime, drugs, etc. that ultimately lead them to social exclusion.

Empowering youth through the right exposure through media at no cost using television and the internet came out to be an imagination turned into reality. All the start up money that she used for this cause was through her line of credit from the bank. But she believed it was all going to come back one day. She invested in the right areas. She even made sure that her team had the right people that could move the project further and improve it continuously with creativity and hard work. She invested time, energy and even money in those people to make them shine because they were all starting out with her. It was a team of talented youth that could see the vision very clearly. Today, her project is well respected and known in the community for its great values.
Learning from the example:

- Know yourself first;
- Have a dream but do not forget the practicality of it. Having a clear vision and mission is very important;

- Research your closest resources first;
- You can't be the master of everything in life, so learn to acquire your resources and let go of control on everything;
- Let your trusted people know about your dream who can support and encourage you;
- Take small steps one at a time to move towards your bigger goal;
- Learn to move ahead by showing gratitude to people who have helped you along in achieving your desires;
- Let there be a team and let the whole team move ahead with you, rise with you because one plus one might not always be two, but it could also, be eleven.

Let's Not Forget the Mentor

One thing that this example did not have was the role of a "mentor". Although, this brave lady mentored her team with her experience but never had her mentor for television production. Her trusted ones did play a collective role as resources in making things possible.

However, having a mentor, a coach in life is sometimes an essential part of the change, right from the transition from who you are to what you want to be.

A coach usually is the one who has been out there doing all, or some part of what you dream of. He is the one, who acts as a guide and makes sure that you are on the right path and doing things effectively. He may not babysit you but open your mind to a plethora of insights that are needed to reach your destination.

So try and make sure that you do have a mentor in your life at least when you are seeking a change and trying to take the first step. If not, it won't be the end of the world. So please don't make this as an excuse for not being able to move forward.

This Is Not A Sacred World- Beware!

One thing that is worth mentioning here is that, if you haven't ever tested the waters with the people you decide to tell your dreams, or the intentions of taking the first step, then better be careful.

"A person should not be too honest. Straight trees are cut first and honest people are screwed first."

~Chanakya

I did mention before that you need to be honest in your endeavors, that means, being honest to yourself. I do not suggest here, especially, with Chanakya's quote above that you should be dishonest with people and simply get your things done. Before I clarify the meaning of this statement, I should explain some more.

Since, today we live in a highly competitive world; a person is most likely understood to be an object of use. Anyone is ready to step onto your head to move ahead. Then why should you act as a fool?

There will be very few, who would actually open the gates of help for you in real terms. Most out there would be much curious to know and gather the ideas and implement them by reinventing the wheel their way, if they like so. Others will most probably discourage you to take that first step trying to make sure you somehow start believing that you are not on the right path. It's all a stupidity that you are going to do; so better stop.

"When most people stamp your intentions to change, your courage, your beliefs and all ideas as invalid and waste; believe me you are already on the road to success."

~Sahil Sharma

Let's Learn the ABC

In your life you will find 3 kinds of people, when it comes to sharing your ideas and looking for resources and encouragement:

- *Mr. A: He, who likes to listen to all you say but dump your ideas right after your mouth shuts by making you focus on your weaknesses and giving you not even a drop of encouragement.*
- *Mr. B: He, who would not even let you complete what you intend to share and pull you down after every second making sure that you believe that you are stupid enough to make a change in your life. He will rather suggest you to do things his way based on completely different ideas.*
- *Mr. C: He, who listens to you and makes sure that you know the pros and cons of your intentions; he, who connects you with resources apart from offering his own*

help along the way; he, who does not feel threatened with your progress in life and rather, likes to open the doors for you.

One common thing in Mr. A and Mr. B is the feeling of jealousy and ego that flashes on their foreheads saying, "We are always right and you are so dumb". Such people are freely available in the world's market. Some interpret it wrongly as competition. While it matters to them or not, such people cannot stand anybody else's progress, whatsoever.

You have to remember that this is not a sacred world, where you would simply go to others and tell about your intentions and you will be helped at once and your story will have a happy ending. Not even Mr. C will be that easy to handle, in case you get lucky finding him because you might not be the ideal Mr. C for him. If you hadn't thought of that yet, then I would like to gift you an alarm clock, so that you can wake up every day with the real facts and get your ideology straight.

Let's be clear on this now. Try to confide into only those that you really feel can help you get on to your endeavors and reach your goals. With rest, who are necessary but not your Mr.Cs, your smartness and selective information sharing will definitely help;

something that does not harm any of the people involved and gets things done.

I Listen To WI FM Everyday! Do you?

I have been a part of different industries in my career; business, radio and television media, social work and hospitality to name them. One of the FM stations that I have always listened to in every industry or say, every part of life is "WI FM". The frequency of this station sometimes is not so clear but what it broadcasts is very clear to understand. I had learnt about this frequency while I studied and worked in the field of marketing. But it has a greater significance in life than just business. WI FM stands for "What's In it For Me". Don't we all ask the same question when someone asks us for help? Then why feel bad, when Mr. C, just in case agrees to help you out, loudly broadcasts this frequency through his actions or words? This is human nature and nothing different.

When you were little and your dad used to ask you to get some groceries from the market, what did you ask for in return? Candy? An extra hour of video games, or maybe a sleep over at your friend's house?

Basically, you broadcasted the same frequency of WI FM to your dad. So you can now understand how a person who is willing to at least help you out still looks for something that can add value to him.

The example that I gave you about my friend, who started her social enterprise, had a similar aspect to it. Her team of youth was looking for something that could add value to their lives and she gave them. Some wanted exposure through the media. Some wanted a boost in confidence. Some wanted to learn more in life. Some just wanted to help because that is happiness for them that adds value to their being. In exchange they offered their resources.

Always remember, this world works on a simple phenomenon of "give and take." Period.

Make sure, when you ask someone to be your resource, you do have something to offer, apart from the fact that your Mr. C will want to go that way, or just be a saint.

There is One Life to Lead

"Trust your instincts, live your values and pursue your own dreams."

~Robin Sharma

At this very stage when some progress has been made, more than that the fear of change and the wind of problems that blow along the journey might make you feel a bit exhausted. Maybe not really exhaustive for some, but for a lot of us that is the word. I am not trying to take you in a fairy world but making you meet the reality. Am I not?

The questions and statements will cloud your mind, "Why do I need to be in all this hassle?" I am okay with what I have. Although, I want to be something else, but it's okay."

We say all this ignoring the fact that every single person on this planet has only one life to live.

"Some choose to be led by their lives and some choose to lead their lives. This is not philosophy".

~Sahil Sharma

This is a reality again. I still remember the words I am writing below resounding in my mind, since I have always felt this and told myself about this repeatedly in life.

"When thinking gets deeper, determination gets weaker."

Thinking to a good and viable extent is healthy but when we start thinking about things too much that need to be done in order to achieve change, then all we do is waste time and energy with no action supplemented. While this waste happens, we also lose determination to do things. As a result, nothing happens and we remain where we were, while achieving nothing.

The BERG Stands Strong!

"He who becomes the BERG can sustain the hits of the ocean and still stand strong."

~Sahil Sharma

Let's see the famous Titanic story with a little different angle. We all know that a berg has the potential to even drown Titanic. Let's change the role of the berg from a villain to a hero in this example. Therefore, the ship becomes the villain that is attacking the hero, the berg.

But the berg remains strong in the cold waters of the ocean, so much so that anything that dares collide with it falls apart.

B: Breaking the box of thinking
E: Ethical & Excellent
R: Responsible
G: Gutsy

The Creation of the BERG- A Leader

Breaking the box of thinking

The world clamors that they need people, who think "out of the box". The question is, "why in the world doesn't somebody break the box?"

Result- No box and a collection of great thinking!

Let me create a definition for you to understand what the phrase, "thinking out of the box" could mean.

"Thinking of breaking the old tried and tested ways with innovation to generate a better impact, increased effectiveness and efficiency of a thing or a process."

Or just,

"Thinking differently."

Therefore, "thinking outside the box" basically reflects creativity.

"Creativity has no rules; that's a rule."

~Sahil Sharma

Creativity is not formed but it forms itself because it emerges from situations, experiences and freedom of thought. Have you ever tried to do the same things that you do every single day in a different way? Have you ever thought of being creative and find solutions to things that bother you choosing another perspective? Have you ever thought of changing your ideas into reality using creativity?

Ask yourself these questions above, and try and get answers. If you haven't done that yet, then start now.

Are You Still "Trying" To Be Creative? Here's a Secret!

There is one important lesson that I wanted you to get, in case by reading all of the above, you were "trying" to be creative and might not have succeeded very well. But I wanted you to at least try first. Now, let me tell you about a secret that really will help you be creative naturally than by just randomly trying to do things differently.

The Secret

In any situation where you are trying to take a different approach has two things attached to it. One is a problem and one is the solution. The problem could not really be a problem but a gap, where some improvement could be made to make things more efficient and effective. The solution is something, where your role comes into play. I am sorry; let me rephrase that, “A genuine solution is something, where your role comes into play.”

I see a lot of people who are very experienced and so called professionals in their work, working on certain guidelines and instructions for years and years. It is not that they are doing something wrong but it has definitely provided them with limited thinking.

In reality, there is no box. Until and unless there is no insightful thinking about what the real problem is, no one can find a real creative and genuine solution.

I remember one day, when I was working at the radio station and making some playlists, I included a song that

I had downloaded online and the playlist editor did not really want to play the song but managed to accept it in the list. When my radio program stopped in the middle when that song arrived, the savaged eyes of my program director were quite a scene to look at. I was told in anger, "nothing like this has happened in years but I do not understand what do you try to do and why can't you follow the instructions".

"Well, I did. It was just a song that I had downloaded from the internet and wanted to play for the listeners; don't know what went wrong. Could you please figure out at least for me?" I continued.

"Ummm…it must be some virus or something. You need to restart the computer and make the whole playlist again", he said.

Guess what? I was not convinced by the answer because it did not make any sense to me, since it was just another song that the playlist could have played. There was no virus, we both knew. My perspective had been different. I did not think about the problem emerging from any virus.

I started with my research to get down to the problem and figured the solution. It wasn't a virus but a simple problem with the format of the song. I managed to change the format of the song with free online software. You know, it did not even cost the radio station anything and I could smoothly play more and better songs then. But I kept it to myself because I anticipated some ego issues. So, I left it to a point of time, when the same thing would happen to someone else and I could then present a solution.

It did happen soon enough with the director one day. Sitting frustrated, he said to me, "What is going on with this stupid software these days. I think I need to update." I used the opportunity to explain things and make everything work smoothly again. The reply from the director, "Interesting, never thought of that."

The moral of the example is simple; learn about the problems first to find solutions that can be creative, while breaking the old conventional patterns.

If many of you think of art and paintings, when you listen to the word "creativity", then let me mention here, that it is an art of finding solutions, or thinking and doing things differently.

If you have understood this well, then you have gained the "B" of the BERG.

Ethical & Excellent

"Being ethical has a simple secret- doing things the absolute right way."

~Sahil Sharma

In a competitive world like today, there will be a thousand obstacles to overcome. No path is straight and easy enough to take, where you can see your goals reached. There will be temptations to do wrong things to achieve goals; the so called short cuts. There will also be ways that are difficult but truly correct and beneficial in the long term. However, the choice remains yours. You can choose to go the wrong way and get things done, or you can choose to go the right way and still get things done.

When you stay ethical in your endeavors, then you are able to influence people more effectively and positively. It can take few seconds to lose all that respect that you might have earned if you turn unethical in your endeavors. For example, a boss, who might pretend to be a leader in his office, asks a subordinate to type something on the computer for him just because he is busy on a personal call. That's unethical.

Remember, a leader or a BERG has its own unique identity that influences people around them. Influence can sometimes backfire, if abused.

If you act ethically, then you will have to think about everyone and not just yourself. Make sure no one gets hurt and everyone gets the benefit. That's the sign of a leader.

"Excellence is doing ordinary things extraordinarily well."

~John W. Gardner

You may be talented enough to be the jack of all trades and master of none. You might actually be really good at doing so many things is all I mean. However, being excellent in just one thing is another sign of a leader. A person can only do things with excellence, when he focuses on something so much that excellence emerges on its own without even knowing.

For example, there was a young boy who used to love cooking and started working in a mall's food court at a Greek restaurant. He used to work hard and you could really see the passion with which he used to cook meals for customers. He used to even talk to them while he cooked, made sure the meats and the breads were cooked properly, food was warm and the drinks were chilled. Extra slices of lemon, or meat well done were things that he remembered for his customers. He even remembered their names. The overall perception of the restaurant went higher in the minds of the customers. They called it "excellent"!

Another thing was noticed there. Whenever that young boy had a day off, the restaurant sales used to get lower than usual. Customers' eyes used to look for him trying to make sure he was working and only after that they would make their way towards the restaurant, or maybe not.

Just a young boy, who was passionate about what he was doing, made his mark in the hearts and minds of so many people. His excellence in doing everything the right way with an extra mile brought the restaurant laurels.

Did people really like the restaurant or the boy's passion of serving great meals with excellence? What to do you think?

Today, the young boy owns his own restaurant and he doesn't mind working with same humbleness and hard work, no matter how many more employees can he afford to bring to serve people. His employees learn from him and he influences them every moment and helps them become the BERG in their own capacities.

Responsible

"Even the spider man knows that with great power comes great responsibility. Why don't we?"

~Sahil Sharma

Being a BERG or a leader is assuming power itself. A berg has the power to influence the direction of the ones coming closer to it. Similarly, a leader has the power to influence people positively and motivate their actions.

Now imagine what a misleading leader can do. It could be a disaster.

In India, there happened to be a self acclaimed saint, who started pretending to be a spiritual leader, who could give solutions to people's problems. Thousands of people started attending his meeting sessions. He would go out to every single province in India and do the same.

Staggering amounts of people were influenced so much that they even forgot to use their own brains.

The so called spiritual leader would give people absolutely bizarre solutions to their problems and people would whole heartedly accept them. It even resulted in someone's death but people ignored because they cared more about their own problems. It did not open their eyes even after the incident. His followers were asked to deposit ten percent of their salaries to his account, if they wanted everything to go the right way. He would audaciously tell people that if they would not deposit money into his account then the solutions suggested will go in vein and stop working for them.

This unethical leader made millions of money with an astonishing annual turnover with his false leadership. He did have the power to influence people using tools such as religion, and so called spiritualism and also the power to abuse it well.

Later, he was caught on cameras by the media and was out to trounce by every action that he took and every word he spoke leading towards blinding people with his false leadership. His own fate seemed to be in jeopardy after trying to change others' destiny.

Learn to act responsibly when you have the power to influence people around. It may take years to reach the ladder of success, glory and whatever comes with it but it will take a few seconds to destroy it all with irresponsible behavior.

Gutsy

"There's a lot of blood, sweat, and guts between dreams and success."

~ Paul Bryant

Only a person who has the courage or the guts to make a change in his life and also in the lives of others can stay strong as a berg. Till the time you don't have the guts to get into the cold waters to stand strong, facing the cold winds and inspire others, you can't move forward in your life trying to change it.

In an example earlier, I had mentioned about the lady who started off her own social enterprise helping younger generation. Imagine if she did not have the guts to really write a proposal for the television program and then take it to the television director. Her dream could never have turned into reality. Imagine, if the very thought of failure could have stopped her from using her own money for starting off the program.

Having guts and believing in your own self goes hand in hand.

Please do not misinterpret having the guts as taking hasty wrong steps on the spur of the moment, or just because you've got some adrenaline rush. Risk taking involves guts. But calculated risk taking is the virtue.

A leader or the BERG will always have the guts to make the change happen with creativity, determination, passion, courage and action, while being ethical and responsible.

Remember, being a BERG doesn't make you less prone to failures. You are allowed to fail as long as you are learning and helping others learn with you effectively.

The Big Shots of the Smaller Moments

I am sure when you hear the word leader, your mind starts reminding you of the great politicians, social workers and even businessmen. However, please know that it is not about having a badge on your shirt or a designation that makes you a leader. I have even seen people at such high designations still not being able to act as leaders.

Have you ever noticed a friend, a colleague or a family member, who always takes the first initiative in doing things in life? For example, a friend who always calls up for a coffee or plans for a picnic, or a colleague, who always speaks his mind in meetings and who is ready to take on some newer roles and take up challenges. All such personalities reflect leadership at whatever level they are at. You really do not need to be called by some special name to be a leader. Your actions will speak for themselves. Try it today at home, at work place and in life genuinely and feel the difference. Every little moment that shines with your leadership can make you a star. You will automatically see the difference with which people act towards you. You know, how people behave differently, when they see the title of a doctor before the name. The respect for that person rises higher, no matter what. You look up to him to save you, or guide you. Similarly, once you get noticed as a genuine leader, you will notice the difference in how you are held in high respect in your life by everyone. Just a little reminder though- Be Responsible.

"Leadership is an art of rising higher in life genuinely and responsibly, while raising others high enough to where you just had been."

~Sahil Sharma

What I have mentioned just above is a reminder about not only leadership but also about the world which is not as sacred as mentioned earlier in the book. Remember? But you have to know that if you are a genuine and responsible leader, it is hard to be replicated by anyone. There has only been one Mozart, one Michael Jackson, one Mahatma Gandhi and there will always be "one you".

I must also mention here about one of the general modern world perceptions of a majority of people. In life, sometimes you do not need to be a PHD graduate, or with some certificates and huge titles to become a leader. It is the understanding of its dynamics and their application that change the perception of a man for himself and in the minds of others. Having knowledge and using the right knowledge at the right time can lead a person to the path of a BERG, or simply a leader.

You Don't Need to Be In Army But Learn To Be A Soldier

"A healthy change needs a healthy you."

~Sahil Sharma

I used to have a bad habit of skipping my breakfast and managing it with a cup of tea and some cookies. I would also not mind to skip my lunch because I was addicted to work and wanted to finish things on time. I would try to do some justice to my body by giving the growling stomach some green tea and maybe some more cookies. Some evening snack and then dinner finally would close my appetite.

Slowly, I realized that my efficiency was going down because I had started feeling tired very early in the day. It would result in less energy, less concentration and work seemed to be like a burden. I had in a way stopped enjoying my work and thinking continuously, what was happening to me.

My boss, who was quite elder to me, said one day, "Right now, I am not your boss. This is like a mother to son talk. You better start eating. Else, it will affect a lot around. You are not going to like it."

With a straight face, I understood what she meant. I started thinking about my daily routine while driving home. I did not find things like exercise, time to relax, and not even proper meals in my life. What else could I expect from my own self? Oh boy, I was going to get into some trouble.

My boss's words resounded in my ears for a few days. I finally got the answer to whatever was happening with me that I didn't like.

The only difference with my boss's lifestyle and mine were some exercise, eating proper meals and some time to relax. Rest we could both perform our jobs well! Guess what? I had to take the first step in this case too, slowly and steadily. If I could not lead myself, how could I even think of positively influencing others?

This is a reminder for all of you, who think that "all work no play", is the key to success. It's not success; it sucks! Just as we demand so many things from our lives, the life also demands a balance from us. This balance is between your work life and your personal life. Please do not leave out the latter behind. Life won't be worth living without that. When you don't supply life with its demands then you spoil the economics yourself here.

You see, the mutual understanding with life doesn’t get developed.

Self discipline is one of those things that can take you far in the race. Giving your life a reasonable schedule might just work out for you. At least give it a try. Certain things need to be in place for a healthy life, so that you have the strength to make healthy changes:

- Positive thinking;
- Right eating habits (consult a dietician);
- Exercise;
- Take out time to relax/pursue your hobbies/listen to music & beat your stress;
- Focus on what you want to do and achieving excellence in it;
- Give time to family and friends;
- Surround yourself with supportive and positive people;
- Avoid negative and discouraging people in life;
- If you can, then spend 15 minutes doing meditation. If you aren’t an atheist, pray and show gratitude towards the universe for whatever you have in life.

Dying Like This? Are You Kidding?

"Don't die a stupid death."

~Sahil Sharma

Imagine, on your journey towards your destination, you get sick just because you did not take care of your health and ultimately, fail to reach where you were supposed to be. Do you afford to be irresponsible then?

I still remember this classmate of mine in high school. He was the topper of the school in every grade. The final year of high school had national examination that really mattered to everyone but I guess, a little more to this gentleman. He literally stopped sleeping at nights but completed every single practice paper that he could. You could see his pale face with big dark eye circles still smiling because he got the answer to the math question first in the class, or knew the capital of some country called Tokelau that no one had ever heard. Unfortunately, when the D-Day came, i.e. Divine day of exams for him, he was admitted to hospital due to some health problems and he could not take any exam. Every one graduated except this gentleman.

Didn't you get the morale of the example by now? I am sure you did.

"You become healthy because your request to the One above to heal your life with great physical and mental strength. Look again, the word is, Heal-Thy. But you've to make the efforts first."

~Sahil Sharma

An individual faces a lot of problems, resistance, obstacles, while in the process of change because accepting it fully as it comes is not so easy. And then, worrying comes naturally to all of us. What does it do though? I personally feel, each time it comes to us; it takes all the positive energy away and fills the emptiness with negative energy. It simply results in low productivity in life, no matter what you do. Your focus wanders; your mental and physical health gets affected. Do you really think worrying is so much worth anyway?

The Woe-Ring- Not a Great Ornament

"Call it woe-ring or worrying, it means the same; an unwanted ring of woes that traps you."

~Sahil Sharma

Worrying is only a trap, or a situation that tests you thoroughly. It challenges you to stay upright strong like a BERG, while it hits you with its cold waves. I like to call such a state of mind, "TIM" that stands for *Temporary Instability of Mind.*
It is a phase in life that makes us go out of character. For example, one day you get laid off from your job and you never had an idea that this was going to happen to you, since you were a really good employee. Everyone liked you and your work at your workplace.

Now, you will suddenly meet Mr. TIM, the one I have mentioned above. He will make you do things that are just not right for you. You will think negatively, as if the world is going to come to an end. How would you pay your bills? How would you keep your family happy? What will you tell your friends? You may have to ask the government for assistance. So many negative thoughts will be brought to your attention by Mr. TIM.

Think about this; if Mr. TIM is not in your favor, then why should you let him enter your life? I have mentioned before, stay away from people who are discouraging and negative in your life. Therefore, learn to practice it, especially, with somebody like Mr. TIM. Try to get back to your basics. Find solutions than focusing on the problems. You will bounce back to a better life faster.

I Told My Mind

While you focus on solutions, you have to tell yourself that everything is temporary, whether good or bad. Nothing shall stay in time. We all know the fact that whatever we tell our mind, it converts it into reality. Don't we?

I still remember a time, when people including some close ones telling me every single time that I was not so ready for the world. I personally have been living away from these people on a journey of my own from higher education and to try making a living based on what my journey taught me. There had been many people and incidences involved that made me learn so much. It was like an on-the-job training of life for me. I am still learning and will always be learning till the end of my last breath. But the very fact that was influencing my mind earlier was the relentless reinstatement of the same words to me, "you are not yet ready for the world".

You know what was happening to me before I took off for my journey? I started believing it slowly. Somebody did say once, "A lie reinstated a hundred times becomes true".

I started feeling all the time that I just wasn't ready for the world. I would fear things and people in life. I felt handicapped and always looked around for people to hold my hand and make me take a step forward. But sometimes, you have to jump into the water to learn swimming yourself because there is a self assurance within that tells you, "You are going to be okay. You can do it. Trust yourself".

Sometimes there won't be a guide, or a teacher but life itself will act as one.

The point that I was trying to make here is to tell your mind whatever you want to achieve in life. Start imagining and living the life you want to have as much as possible for now. It will automatically prepare your mind for the best. You will start creating your future now. Some people call it "affirmation". I just call it a "mind-talk". So, take the opportunity today to tell your mind what you want and start working on it with your actions. This beautiful combination will work wonders! Remember, this is not overnight magic. It is a process that you will start now to build tomorrow. There will be failures and successes and the only thing that will keep you motivated is your imagination of being where you want to be with great determination. Imagine the people, who are already there and then, keep your own self in the same position. Don't you really want to be there? Act on it slowly and steadily- one step at a time.

Two Ends of the Rope

Life is like a two ended rope that you walk on to get to the other side, while trying to balance yourself, so that you don't fall. Nobody in this world can deny the fact that life is full of only one thing, either happiness, or sadness. They both have their own beautiful roles to play that make us feel balanced in life. Without having to know one of them, we won't be able to appreciate the other.

In many religious holy books such as Bhagwad Gita, these have been termed as the "Pair of Opposites". In simple terms, once the person learns to disconnect himself from the pair of opposites and rather focuses on doing things correctly, or basically, doing his karma, then automatically, the life starts following a healthy path. For example, if someone works hard enough to get something he really wants without thinking what the results of his hard work might be, he could actually create success for himself. However, even if not, he shall have little disappointment but an appreciation towards the learning process that he went through and a motivation to move forward for his betterment.

I am not trying to teach religion here at all. That is not my motive. My only motive is to get across a simple point, that is, working towards the goal is more important than worrying about the results all the time. Worries will only let you be inefficient than what your real potential is. If you don't believe it, then try it sometime. Consciously watch yourself, or someone close to you, who is falling into the trap of worrying. You will definitely have your answer.

We had talked about responsibility earlier. One of the most important responsibilities towards your own self is to keep yourself healthy. Don't you think so? If you can't lead your life in a healthy way, then how can you lead by example for others? Remember, any change that is desired by you does not only bring change to your own life but also to the environment affecting it.

When Fear Shows You the Way Ahead

"Fear is like a spear that either pierces our goals leaving us with holes, or cuts a way ahead of us to help us prepare for the best and the worst."

~Sahil Sharma

I do not remember even a single person in my life that has not shown any sign of fear, when going through some change or taking the first step towards it. Do you still remember the fear of accepting that you were going to go to a higher grade after you pass the one you were in? Do you remember submitting your exam well but still fearing a lower grade? Do you remember about the fear of separating from a loved one, thinking that your relationship will never be the same?

So many examples could be derived from our daily lives where we all resonate. Fear is a very common emotion which has its own special place in life.

"The feeling of being uneasy or uncomfortable thinking of the unknown yet to be, describes fear."

~Sahil Sharma

Had we as human beings could know everything that was coming in every second of our lives, there would have been no fear, or may be very less because the chance of being prepared would have been much higher along with the certainty of the future. We could have been secretaries to God. Don't you think?

Fear is both, healthy and unhealthy. I understand that the latter seems to be very obvious. Let's discuss it more simply using an example. Will you work all the same way in your office, if there was no fear of your boss, or fear of losing your job, if you did not perform well? I personally do not think so. Quite normally, once the boss is out of the office, most of us feel at ease. We even like to check our Facebook accounts quickly or just have a quick chat with our colleague. Now imagine if every day was the same for you. Where will the productivity of the company go? Get into the shoes of your boss and just think once.

Another example could be of people who fear the almighty, the God. It helps them fear the results of bad karma. Whatever you throw out towards the universe, the gravitational force will bring it back to you in some way. At least that is what I believe. Therefore, it becomes essential for such people to stay good to everyone and try to do good deeds as much as possible.

In both the examples above, I have suggested that some fear that results in a good and positive environment of your existence is healthy.

Now let's take one more example. A person named Steve, who has all great educational degrees in hand, feels that he gets underpaid but at the same time doesn't want to change his job. He thinks it is too much of an effort. He will have to go for interviews, maybe sit at home for few months jobless and all other uncomfortable things that might be a part of the transition will follow. Basically, there is a problem and there is also a solution. But the fear of going through the change and taking a step forward is bringing no results to Steve. A talented person is frustrated even after having some great talents and skills that can help him achieve what he wants in life.

Then I also see people who have no legs or arms and still making stories around the world and inspiring million others through their courage. They beat fear off. That word is such a waste of energy.

"You know, no one likes the F word. It just wastes energy. I hate Fear too that is unhealthy."

~Sahil Sharma

Such fear is disastrous for man. Not being able to motivate himself to accept some discomfort to reach the most comfortable zone he wants to be in. This could be lack of confidence, lack of motivation, lack of resources, or simply procrastination. That is why it was mentioned earlier in the book that let the most positive supporters be with you and know what you wish to achieve. Their words of encouragement and wisdom many times act as that "one push" that you need to get your life rolling.

Procrastination is the biggest enemy of transformation and progress. If you keep procrastinating, then things will all be messed up and you will end up dissatisfied with the results of what you were trying to achieve.
On the contrary, some people use fear as a tool to complete things faster, or do a better job. It helps them fight procrastination. Such people understand their own selves and use this tool to their advantage. For example, a person has some fear of losing his job. Whenever, he

does not perform to a basic level, he reminds himself of his fear, in order to perform better. It works as some kind of motivation for him. I call this "healthy fear". Healthy fear only sets in when you need to get something done with its limitations, such as time. It does not hang in the brain 24/7 as a life taking stress. It is just momentary. Such fear helps a person to stay on the track of life.

Therefore, keep yourself restricted to healthy fear and live in the present.

"The faster you face your fears; lesser the time will you take to reach success."

~Sahil Sharma

One of the most important things to learn about fear and put into practice is to get rid of it soon. If you fear something, or something is worrying you, then try and get those things out of the way first. John is worried about his assignment which is due day after tomorrow but he is just fearful enough not to touch it and drag the assignment to the very last moment, when he will have no choice but to complete it in a rush. He doesn't realize, if he could do such an assignment first, then he could give his mind rest, or do something that he likes with no worries in mind.

More simply, imagine you are scared of spiders and one day you happen to see it right in front of your face, while entering your room. Your reaction? You will try to kill it, or just get rid of it somehow as fast as possible. Similar logic should apply to other fears in life too that you know you are facing, or you will have to face soon enough. Face it today, face it now and feel better.

Another example could be of a group discussion. You must have noticed that some people have that anxiety about them speaking in front of a group. You will also notice people who build the platform for discussion with their own perspectives by speaking first. Those people act as leaders by taking the initiative of doing their acts faster and giving no time to fear to set it.

Every individual needs to be a leader of his own path. Let fear be a tool of strength that can make you rise higher just like an eagle, which starts flying higher at the time of storms, whereas all other birds find their hiding places.

The Fear Magnets

You will someday realize that certain characters around you fear happiness. Sounds strange? Have a look around again. May be you do too. I call them the *fear magnets* or the *worry magnets*. Such people tend to find worries and fears in their lives. No offence to anyone but that is their nature, either by default, or due to some learnt behavior in family, or friends that acts in a similar way. They can't believe in themselves that they could be happy too. They become cry babies and can't see happiness whatsoever. As soon as they see some trouble coming, they naturally feel that there is a job for them to combat. It empowers them in some sense. The fear of trouble keeps their mind busy. Although, they will never agree with you on this but this is somehow an observation that holds true for me. The question here is, why some people become fear magnets?

Is something wrong with them?

I don't think so. The only missing piece is the understanding of the dynamics of this universe. I had mentioned earlier in the book about "WI FM", or What's In it For Me. This is a simple give and take process. You give something to someone to receive something in return and it balances out the whole

equation. Similarly, whatever you give back to your environment, it simply gives you back the same. When the environment asks you about WI FM, you give worries and fear to it and it automatically returns you the same. This is not philosophy of any kind. This is practical truth; as much truth as needing water when you are thirsty. It is just natural. When people see that their fear is converting into truth that was uncertain before, but certain now, they become more worried and anxious and the whole vicious circle continues.
I will leave you with two questions- What will happen, if you always think of the good things? Don't you think they can be provided to you by your environment, or the universe? Can't you become "happiness magnets"?

Are You Breathing Right Now?

Can you please stop doing whatever you are doing for a minute and check if you are really breathing? Can you feel your breath moving in and out of your body? Can you feel your heart beating? Now think about this. You breathe every day, every second of your life but never stopped for a second to make sure you were really breathing or not. You were much more focused, either on the past, or the future. We forget that every present moment was once future and future will once become the past. If you focus on the present, or the "now" and make efforts in making it better, then automatically things of the past and future will be the way you have always wanted.

If Michael starts worrying about his tomorrow's meeting in the office and stops focusing on the meeting that he is attending "now", then he will not be able to absorb what was required from the current meeting and automatically, generate problems for himself for the next meeting. If a college student starts dreaming that he will be a doctor one day and stops focusing on what his lectures are teaching him in his college, then neither will he learn anything, nor will he be able to become a doctor. If Marie has just had herself a job but instead of being happy, she keeps on thinking about her position in the company in the next 2 years, then she will lose the happiness that a new job can get. Ignoring happiness and the present cannot help you being a strong and focused individual. Stop worrying, or fearing what has not happened yet, or what has already happened. Both the situations are out of control.

Filling Your Mind with What Is Needed

"Mindfulness is realizing the present existence."

~Sahil Sharma

One day, I found my favorite CD of songs in my room. Seeing the music player in front of me, I was tempted to insert the CD and play a nice song for myself. I did. My eyes had already closed as my heart and mind were excited to listen to the song and get some relaxation out of it.

The song started and 20 seconds passed. My mind started wandering, thinking about the events of the past and worries about the future events. My mind was so engrossed that I did not even realize that the 6 minute long song had already passed and the CD had stopped. Nowhere close did I get to what I was wishing to achieve.

In simple words, I was not aware of the present moment and I was more engrossed in thinking about something else that was occupying my mind.

This is a mind with no mind or mindlessness. Had I paid attention to the song by being aware that I was listening to it, it would have given me what I had expected, i.e. relaxation. That would have been a mind with a mind or mindfulness.

Have you ever forgotten the names of people as soon as they introduce themselves? Have you ever worked like a robot without even realizing what you were doing and why? Have you ever eaten snacks just because you wanted to and never realized that your stomach was actually full? Have you been occasionally called "careless" by others?

Don't worry, being mindless is very common. We all are in that state most of the time. Mindfulness requires some conscious effort though. But we are too busy judging the moments that have either passed, or not have even become the part of our existence. We forget to recognize the environment that we are living in the present.
I usually go to my work place using the same route for the last 2 years. I was looking for a jeweler shop one day and just couldn't figure out whom to go to. My mother suggested the jeweler that comes on the way to my office.

"Oh really? Which one is that, mom? I asked.

Mother said, "Don't you see it always? It's the very first shop with so many fancy lights flashing."

Had I paid attention to the things that come in my way to the workplace, I could have avoided the worry of finding a jeweler at the time I needed. Since I did not, I was anxious enough to find one that suited my needs.

If we keep our minds awake and pay attention to what we do and what is happening inside and outside of our existence, then we can even recognize the feeling of fear and combat it well within time. Being mindful helps a person to know who they are, and what they are doing and why. I would actually believe that a person who is mindful has the greatest potential to achieve success in whatever form because he will know what he is doing.

It comes back to the same point that I have been trying to make earlier in this book, i.e. living in the present.

Please do not confuse mindfulness as something against focusing on life. I am sure a lot of you who are reading this right now are thinking that why in this world is this author confusing us. Should I be focusing on the task that I am doing completely, or not?

Focusing on one thing at a time that is a part of the steps you take to achieve your goals, also requires mindfulness. If you are focusing on completing the assignment that you dislike first in order to get rid of your anxiety quickly, then you will need to be aware of the reason of why you are completing this particular assignment first. Also, you will need to know what actions you would choose and what will the results be, while heading towards its completion.

Focusing is therefore, giving direction to your mind for a purpose. Mindfulness is following the direction by being aware of the purpose, recognizing it and paying attention to the inside and outside of your existence, while you focus.

All of us should be aware of the feelings that we go through every second, whether good or bad. Only after you recognize your feelings consciously, can you act on them appropriately by taking the required action. Recognizing fear, as an example, is therefore, very important to take an action at the right moment to combat it faster.

Think of your situation like a movie that you are watching. Be the director first and then become an actor. Once you learn to detach yourself from the situation for a while and give yourself a chance to think rationally, then you will be able to see things more clearly. Clarity of mind will definitely result in clarity of action

The Day Shall Come...

"Hope is the rope of our existence on which we walk every day. Looking down won't help but looking forward will help you balance and cross the distance between where you are and where you want to be."

~Sahil Sharma

One thing that keeps us all going even in the worst situations of life is hope. Hope is an unfulfilled expectation, which carries some positivity in itself and keeps individuals motivated. Hope helps bring the level of worry down, since it is a positive affirmation that your wish might come true.

Hope usually comes with an element called faith; faith in your own self and faith in the Almighty. Although, both fear and faith give you feelings of nervousness due to the component of uncertainty but both ultimately move in different directions. Faith moves upwards and uplifts you too. Fear moves downwards and leads you towards the bottom of your worth. Fear lets opportunities pass by and faith lets you try out the opportunities and move with a feeling of accomplishment ahead. When I say the word "accomplishment", then I mean the steps taken forward towards the opportunities. The result has no significance in this journey because it is a journey of experience that may lead to success, or something else that can open other beneficial doors for you.

Choosing faith over fear is sometimes a need than a choice. So, make a good choice when choosing and understanding your need.

Attitude towards Change

"Life is like a scene of your own movie that you want to capture. You only see what you want from behind the lens. Change the scene, if you don't like it, or be the editor to bring the change in the same scene to make it all good."

~Sahil Sharma

You must have heard the very old story told to you by your parents or grandparents about seeing a glass half full or half empty. It's not that we don't know it but we constantly need reminders in life for the things that we know but forget.

After understanding about the environment of change, you would know that the process of change is not so pleasant for everyone. As I had mentioned before, a lot of negative thoughts will appear in your mind and a lot of people around you will try to discourage you as well. But remember, you've got to be the BERG. In our lives, we always remember some things said by somebody close to us. I also remember something said to me by someone close. He said, "Listen to everyone but do what you think is right". That is how my life works even today. It is important to have all the perspectives in mind because they help you find the best solutions in life but they are definitely not stated to you as the final words of wisdom. Use your facts and then listen to your inner self to walk on the path that you may choose as correct for your life.

That's not all. There are some key things to remember that become your attitude towards change in life:

Gratitude: Always thank the universe for whatever it has provided you with. Pause your life for a minute and think about those, who starve for a single grain of rice, or a drop of water in some parts of the world. Don't you think you are way better off? I am sure you will feel better after giving it a thought. Thank people, who try and help you during your journey towards your life. Without them, it could have been a different story.

Focusing On What Needs To Be Done: Finding solutions is the key to end the problems. Focus on what you have right now and what can be done with what you have. Crying, or thinking over what you do not have is a waste of energy and time. They will lead you nowhere. Never include statements like, "I could have been, or it could have.." in the dictionary of your life because they really have no meaning anymore. So what's the point of focusing on them?

Taking Right Actions at the Right Time: Thinking about change, making plans, and day dreaming does not help in realizing your dreams. Only action towards achieving them at the right time makes the difference. Take steps and you will automatically run as the path unfolds.

Understanding Change: Accepting change and taking time to understand the process to see things clearly is very important. Remember, you won't know about the results, unless you make the change. Be patient and see the difference for your own betterment. A farmer can't expect to have the fruits of the plant today that he has seeded a day ago. Even a child takes 9 months in the womb of a mother to get in to this life. During that process, the mother gives the child nourishment, so that the child is born healthy. Same goes with the farmer. Quitting or giving up during the process of change with some failures may act as tides that will try to hit you many times. But a BERG, i.e. "you", will need to let them flow back into the ocean. These are just momentary. They cannot break you down because you are stronger in time than these little moments.

"The right attitude is the way to go! It is also the way to come back and start again."

~Sahil Sharma

Be Your Own Fan!

"To be a great champion you must believe you are the best. If you're not, pretend you are."

~Muhammad Ali

Although, this is also a part of the attitude that should be adopted in life, I wanted to bring this one out separately. Ask yourselves right now, "Are you proud of whatever you do the best in life?"

It is very important for us to love and respect our own selves first in order to give the same out to others. When I used to run restaurants, I always would remind my employees of one thing. I would say, "If the food that you are serving your customers doesn't tempt you, or make you feel like the master chef while cooking, then the food is not worth serving". Today, they understand this well. It is a part of them.

It is not that they can compete against the best in the world but they definitely are the heroes of their kitchen. You can see the spark in their eyes when they are cooking with pride and the love for food and serving others. They work hard at it.

Once you become the master chef in your own kitchen as well, then nobody in the world can cook the way you do.

Look at yourself in the mirror everyday for a minute, pause your life for a minute and see if there is anyone else like you out there. I know the answer, “I don’t think so”.

"Every single life that we live has its own unique story; as unique as we are."

~Sahil Sharma

Now that you have been reminded of some essentials of an ever changing life, what are you thinking about?
Take a deep breath, smile and start now.

This is not a book that is influenced by a thousand other books. Every word of this book has come from the life and experience of what I have learnt, felt and wanted to share with all of you reading it. Life has its turns and twists and brings us at a point in time, where everything seems to have come to a stop. For all those I could help in moving further in life by taking a step forward, I appreciate and respect their dreams, actions & accomplishments.

Sahil Sharma

Author

www.ingramcontent.com/pod-product-compliance
Ingram Content Group UK Ltd.
Pitfield, Milton Keynes, MK11 3LW, UK
UKHW020218250726
13967UKWH00001B/63
9 781105 789106